Lit Only by a Few Thousand Stars

Poems by
Anna Kodama

BLUE LIGHT PRESS ◆ 1ST WORLD PUBLISHING

SAN FRANCISCO ◆ FAIRFIELD ◆ DELHI

Winner, 2023 Blue Light Book Award
Lit Only by a Few Thousand Stars
Copyright ©2023, Anna Kodama

All rights reserved. Printed in the United States of America. No part of this book may be used or reproduced in any manner whatsoever without written permission except in the case of brief quotations embodied in critical articles and reviews. For information contact:

BLUE LIGHT PRESS
www.bluelightpress.com
bluelightpress@aol.com

1ST WORLD PUBLISHING
PO Box 2211
Fairfield, IA 52556
www.1stworldpublishing.com

BOOK & COVER DESIGN
Melanie Gendron
melaniegendron999@gmail.com

COVER ART
Through Dark Phases of the Moon by Anna Kodama

INTERIOR ILLUSTRATIONS
Anna Kodama

AUTHOR PHOTO
Janine Feeney

FIRST EDITION

ISBN: 978-1-4218-3535-8

Library of Congress Cataloging-in-Publication Data

Lit Only by a Few Thousand Stars

Anna Kodama

Contents

The Weight of Missing Mountains

How Can Your Absence Be So Present? 1
Catch and Release 2
Cast Away 4
Geologic Nonconformity 5
How Many Eels Does It Take to Make a Lasting Landscape? . 6
A Hundred Days 8
Let Me Tell You Why 9
Via Negativa of a Noonday Walker 10
Labyrinth 11
A Natural History of Metamorphosis and Decay 12
Relativity 13
The Museum of Birdsong 14
Plattekill Travel Plaza 15

When the Carrier Wolves Come

Wolf Rock 19
In Sleep, Some Promise Kept 20
Barefoot in the Dust of a Dream 21
Shining Cloistered Silence 22
The Wolf's Testimony to the Mother 23
Homeostasis 25
Naming the Birds 26
Passing Through on Your Way 28
Last Night, the Tree of Life 30
Sophia, Awake in the Middle of the Night 32
What Is Your Name Before You Are Born? 34
Persephone's Return 35

Light Strikes the Bell of the Heart

"You've Reached Peter. Please Leave a Lengthy Message!" ... 41
Oriole Nest 42
Cerulean Window, Maybe a Door 43
In Your Shoes 44
Coyote's Return 45
To the Vulture in Search of a Dead Groundhog 46
Silent Retreat 47
Gaia's Prayer 49
Sleeping All Night on the Dock 50
Windless Night in the Forest 51
Night Life 52

A and B Blown Out to Sea

Arctic Prayer 55
After a Great Storm 56
Endless as an Arctic Winter Night 57
Winter's Wise Counsel 58
Night Before the Last Ship Sailed 59
We Are More and Less Than We Know, and Braver Too 60
Early Morning in the Studio 61
Song of the Hag 62
Last Day on Hrísey 64

From Earth to the Separating Stars

To the Grandchildren 67
Here, Now 68
Evidence 69
Prayer of the People 71
Ocarina 72
About That Thought Experiment by Schrödinger 74
Mudstone Speaks to the Mother of Matter 76
The Message 79
Not Yet 80

Old Love Knits a Sweater

Here, in the City 83
Old Love Knits a Sweater 84
Time Travel 85
Animal Soul Longing 87
The Union of Two Rays at a Vertex 88
Left at the Altar of Undigested Light 89
Returning to the Labyrinth After Weeks in the City 90
Where the Old Dog Dozed 91
Maybe This Is Why I Married You 92
Field Assistant 94
Ipiutaq, Greenland 96

Acknowledgments 98

About the Author 99

For Peter

Morning Glory's Prayer
Through the Dark Phases of the Moon

Invisible Mother Drum
Incomprehensible Earth Mover
Sea Sweller
Fish Feeder
Ineluctable Time Keeper.
Tonight, the jealous Father of all Light
hoards your reflection
on the far side of the world,
but he's powerless to stop your circle dance.
All night I hear you.
Just before dawn,
when the sweep of your skirt
brushes my hips,
your perfume fills my throat.
Your song,
my one breath,
broadcasts before the birds,
for the glory of deep violet nights
lit only by a few thousand stars.

The Weight of Missing Mountains

How Can Your Absence Be So Present?

I wouldn't expect you to linger in the garden
as you did when you were little,
or stay home playing fiddle in the D Minor Duo.
You'd probably move far away
with some career,
your crazy songs sung for friends,
and maybe a lover we haven't met.

If you called, I'd tell you I'm planting Little Marvel peas,
and when I pick them in 60 days,
we will deliver a luscious bagful.
Your dad will bring new strings for your instruments.
I will ask you to stoop so I can kiss the top of your head
before you split open the pods and eat.

Not that it would be like this.
Not that it would be like anything.
It would just be today –
this first blue sky spring morning
when each turning shovelful of dark earth
is warmer than the last.

Catch and Release

> ...a *Beautiful Nothing.*
> *Deserving a capital letter.*
> *– Wislawa Szymborska*

The baby you are nursing arches his spine
and turns into a fish.
You wake up still human.
Your most tender skin
not even scratched by his rigid dorsal
or bruised by the muscular slapping tail.

Nothing remains
but sloughed-off moonlit scales
in a dusty corner of blue linoleum.

Nothing in the birch wood cradle
carved from a single burr.

Long ago, you learned to stand on mother's lap.
You walked on solid ground,
your own sweat perfuming the air,
your feet cracked and brimming
with flecks of cosmic dust.

When saltwater poured out of your womb,
a sweet grass world was born,
milking your breasts,
rejoicing flesh to flesh.

But you have swum enough New Hampshire ponds
to remember water
and the warm granite boulders where you stretched.

Now in this predawn hour,
with the hook in your tongue,
you recall the body's dark silhouette
the moment before it evaporates
in the sun.

Cast Away

With a family in a house on a street
where kids built forts from curbside leaves,
and rode thick-tire bikes home before dark.
Our driveway gravel held tiny stones that spoke.
They told me you'd be coming,
born from a blue mare or a mountain,
inside a world away.

They never said I'd be gone,
adrift in my own high-sided wooden boat
upon a latent glassy sea.
Ghosts rise in smoke from far-off burning bushes.
Old women listen in their shuttered rooms
for someone on the stairs.
My vessel rocks beneath its aimless boom,
the heavy canvas sail a swaying wall
separating nothing.

No fish jump.
No islands interrupt.
Oh gray and starless night,
without angels or a Jonah whale!
Don't let me be where you are not.
Bring this body's bones
your breath, your light.

Geologic Nonconformity

We are swimming in a waterless ocean,
belly down, naked and shivering
on the vast Gatineau bedrock north of Ottawa.

A thick blanket of loam and hemlock forest
has rolled back, exposing dinner-plate-sized fossils
dredged from the ancient sea,
and stained by blue-green algae
that lost their color
when they clung and turned to stone.

Ridges scrape our palms and elbows raw,
but we cannot seem to free ourselves –
to push off from this four-billion-year-old reef
and stand with our faces toward the trees.

The weight of missing mountains
presses down.
Stunning, snow-peaked Himalaya
rose, fell and vanished here
while our molecules dreamed the deep time.
Now our hands slide
across the limestone mattress,
every pore in our body
searching for a smooth depression,
a warm and familiar well to curl into.

What sort of lover
slips out in the Precambrian dawn?
What sort of mother
abandons her children
before they've even met?

How Many Eels Does It Take to Make a Lasting Landscape?

I didn't know eels live in Durham Creek
until a posse of naturalists waded upstream,
zapping the water with battery-powered wands
that beeped like cicadas.

With a little electricity,
you can immobilize fish
long enough to count and measure
before they swim away.
Dazed minnows and brook trout float into your net.
Sleek yellow elvers uncurl in the silt
and lie like pencils on a plate.
Their length and numbers prove the water pure enough
to certify a Lasting Landscape.

I used to walk the banks of that crooked stream
with a five-year-old kid,
his boots and plastic bucket.
He dragged a stick through the water,
flipping over rocks, reaching under logs,
trapping whatever wriggled through his fingers,
and pouring them all back
before the long walk home.

Home is a thing you teach your kids –
the fox in his den, bird in her nest,
boy in a gray clapboard house
with his mother and father.

If you didn't teach home,
would they ever know?
First drawings are portraits of the self.
A child's eyes look out a circle face.

The tiny crooked rectangle of home
crawls later from the crayon box
to lean on a wobbly line
at the very bottom of the page.

Now they have found these eels,
but the naturalists worry they will not stay.
We need to keep them
fifteen or twenty years, an age
to swim down the Delaware River,
across the Atlantic Ocean
3000 miles, to breed and die
in the green Sargasso Sea
where they were born.

When someone leaves
his muddy boots to dry
and makes an impossible journey
from which he never returns,
can the Lasting Landscape
still be home for the rest of us?

A Hundred Days

Your brown and green sneakers wait on the porch.
Last summer's fishing pole behind the door
where Rudy's tail gets it every time.
Four-leaf clover pressed into so many books,
luck falls out every time we turn a page.

Fiddle strings wound in perfect circles.
Your good bow re-haired by David Michie.
Tickets to see the Dalai Lama –
not exactly an audience with God,
but still.

Your phone holds messages we can't unlock.

We have being here
and hearing, growing, tasting, touching.
Singing harmony.
Swallowing the bread I've baked.

Becoming.
Are you?

Let Me Tell You Why

I went into the tangled wood,
took a hatchet to the bittersweet
and multiflora rose,
and yanked the twisted honeysuckle
until its trailing vines snapped.

I battled these invaders for days,
to find the old wall buried underneath.

In grief,
stones satisfy.

Rough mica schist,
age-spotted, frost-cracked
chunks of iron ore, and limestone.
I tore into this uneven cast-off rubble
while the casseroles piled up in the kitchen,
and cards with angels on the shelf.

I lifted, slammed, kicked, heaved.
I shook off red ants,
thousand-leggers and pill bugs.
I jammed my fingers into the gaps
and pried apart the heavy slabs,
ripping away soft moss
and musty nets of mycelium
to free the hard, enduring bones
of this sweet earth.

Via Negativa of a Noonday Walker

Here is what I didn't see:
The five-point buck and albino doe
in Torpee's Woods.
The bald eagle
or any sharp-shinned, red-tailed,
broad-winged bird of prey
patrolling the warm updrafts
above the power cut.

No blue heron in the dead ash tree,
woodchucks among the hay bales,
mallards, Canada geese,
or cellophane-winged dragonflies
lapping the slick muddy cow pond.
No sign anywhere
of three black bears
that woke Dee Brothers after midnight,
then lumbered back to the woods.

Cloudless white with no sun,
the poetry of no encounter
isn't spare or clean.
It doesn't write itself
on an absent sky,
but speaks in every footstep
of the noonday walker.

Labyrinth

They were just rocks
until crowbarred out of the earth
and brushed clean.
When I placed them
in a keyhole spiral
on a smooth sea of river gravel,
poured and spread over a wide clearing
prepared long ago
by a boy,
as a place to watch deer,
they became sentries.
Witnesses. Stones
anyone can walk between
and turn into prayer.

A Natural History of Metamorphosis and Decay

The cherry aims to save her wood for caskets
and shed desire with her leaves,
but what feeds on heartwood
erupts along the spine.
Shelves of wrinkled fungus
build a golden stairway
invoking angels.

They swarm on holy wings
with star-forged swords
that loose the fragrant bark.
Blessings break like ocean waves
against the naked trunk
until every walled cell sings
to the longhorn beetle deep within.

"Do you mean me?"
the clawed and newly armored Jacob asks.
"Do you mean now?"

We burrow and chew,
nursing our soft-bellied hungers
and spiraling questions
until the cocoon splits open.
We can shrivel and hide
in the rotting husk
or step out on the tip
of a vanishing sword,
freed from our history,
alive in the light blind silence
of angel feathers and fallen trees.

Relativity

Fifty years ago to pass the test,
I memorized the constellations
according to the buildings
on Mount Holyoke's campus.
At half past seven in mid-November,
Cassiopeia was shining three thumbs left of Abbey Hall.
The Great Bear rose above the chapel tower.

But stars can lose their gods,
let go their myths,
and strand us in the spaces in between.

What I know of night,
I learn while sleeping on my back
in a clearing beside the stone labyrinth
built with my own hands
in the middle of a forest
of ailing ash trees and broken too-tall poplars.
All around me, beneath the dark dome sky,
animals I cannot see to name
shine their eyes and snuffle,
grunt, and cry.

The Museum of Birdsong

Suddenly, in the Museum of Birdsong,
I remember the brightness of his flaxen hair.
How my boy lit the nursery room himself.
As himself.
That was why he could not sleep.
Could not lie still in his crib.
Had to hoist himself over the railing,
patter around the braided rug in his footed pajamas
and climb the creaking rocker, horsehair stool
and armchair where he dangled
from one upholstered wing
to the other.

I had witnessed everything
except the Disappearance.
Replacement. Transformation
from small, kinetic light boy
to dazzling, moonfaced barn owl.
Stillness on soft feathered legs.
Pale toes curled over the headboard
with its cutout Peter Rabbit.

No sound.
This is what I both remember
and learn
in the hushed velvet galleries
of the Museum of Birdsong.
Where all the docents are deaf,
and their nimble white-glove hands
arrange the air –
their palms upon my chest,
their fingers fluttering
my lips.

Plattekill Travel Plaza

How many pieces of myself did I give away,
not to be guilty, not to be alone?
At a highway rest stop
in the traffic for the toilet,
I see an old woman with her green comb
and her eyes on the mirror over the sink.
My hand grips the grimy faucet
stuck between off and on.
The dribble of rusty water
barely wets the tips of my fingers,
yet it leaves them numb.
The ceiling bulb chirps a shaky blue light.
The faltering incandescence
burns all the forests I have ever known
and the children I have loved.
When the old woman is gone,
I am too.
Out from the buzz of this moment,
tracking her long cloud shadow
into the night.

When the Carrier Wolves Come

Wolf Rock

We were staying at a rooming house
in the low, snowy hills of the Hasliberg.
It was my dream,
but you were there with your sisters.
All of us took the rough stone steps
down to the village of lighted windows
casting squares of gold and lavender
on the icy streets.
Cats, plump as pillows, slept in the alleys
and a crackling radio played for dancers
round an oil drum fire.

Somehow you ran ahead.
The toe of your boot landed
in a circle of street light,
your face in shadow.
You bent forward,
scooping snow, shaping it as you rose,
drawing back in a single balletic gesture
that sent the snowball sailing
into a blue black
no-stars, nameless night
that swallowed you again.
And set me down in summer.
Awake on these high broken rocks,
my hands lifted,
anxious to catch
what you so boldly threw.

In Sleep, Some Promise Kept

When the Carrier Wolves come,
nothing can stop us from falling like water on their backs.
We bury our cheeks in their fur and breathe in the forest.
Our fists clutch the silken folds behind their ears.
Knees on either side squeeze their flanks,
as our soft human belly sinks into the swaying spine.
No one has to teach us how to ride.
We learned the smooth animal maneuvers
before our birth, before our eyes,
when we still had tails and nothing to hide.

Something about our bodies now,
and the uneven ground of lives lived in electric cities,
has caused us to forget the ancient promise –
the treaty lost in shame and ashes long ago.
The other party vanished from our midst,
but the loyal wolves of the Carrier Clan
insist that darkness will not be a shroud.
They sneak into our palaces and prisons,
lift us from our bed of roses or nails
and carry us like cargo,
on a zigzag path between the trees,
across the wind-stripped plains,
up through the glacial scree of a high mountain pass.
They deliver us to the shore of an endless lake
where we throw stones at our reflections,
and try in vain to wake the Creator
from his mud bound sleep.

Barefoot in the Dust of a Dream

A paddy wagon unlocks its hinged back.
Ropes untie themselves, and I slide down
into warm grey ash, my legs already running.
By day, I'm a fugitive on the open road,
a victim of the man in snakeskin boots.
Tonight, I'm an athlete,
alone in a race with no competitors.

The air is not good.
Each footfall into soft dust releases a puff of smoke.
Words drift from my pockets.
Who made this course? Did my father run it?
My mother? My boy? They are gone
and I am padding deeper into my own dust.

A dry world coats my hair and tongue
with talc and mica sparks of stars I cannot see.
I am far from the city of holy faith,
the blood mountains, the green turtle sea.

But my body hums in this closed circuit.
My heart gallops.
Like a ribbon on a wheel,
the track unrolls
from the muscles of my legs.
There is nowhere but here.
An invisible gaze holds me like a kite.
At my breast,
a long taut string.

Shining Cloistered Silence

Liquid light melts
the elephant skin branches
of an old beech tree.
Ropes of golden rain
stream through my hair.
I stand with the blue mare
in her paddock
where the whole world,
without reservoir or wellspring,
empties itself.

No pipes or pumps or hidden spigots.
Nothing to open or to close.
A black carriage faces the fence,
its canvas curtains zipped tight from inside.
A lanky child barnacles to her mother's hip.
A soldier grips his automatic.
A clown juggles fire and knives.
I stand with the blue mare.

The Wolf's Testimony to the Mother

When the incubating dream
containing us whole as an egg
shattered that night,
you woke in dry leaves and broken branches.

You cried out,
"I will not let you go!"

Your words broke the night.
Arms flew out,
fingers stretching like a newborn's
into empty air,
missing me by just a hair.

You, the cargo on my back,
the sleeping infant – girl – woman
I had carried to the lake
night after night,
lowered into the eider boat
and waited on shore
till dream-fed you rode me home.

What could you know of me?

But the pores of your skin
must have brimmed
with my rank oil.
Your hips, ribs and belly charged
with my bounding stride,
my breath and heartbeat
driving yours.

You tore into the dark
in just the right direction,
tracking me, as sure as any wolf.
You, only a woman
in her nightgown,
running on two legs
and tender human feet.

Homeostasis

I dreamed about a peacock with rabies.
The next morning, painting this bird
through a keyhole,
I became the only witness
to its miraculous restoration.
The gasping beak hinged shut
and swallowed the angry foam.
The limp crest twitched
as its blue feather flowers
sprang to life on wiry stems,
instantly galvanizing
the scabby piebald head
and electroplating every feather
with the smooth iridescent
enamel shine
of a lapis-colored
Roman centurion helmet.

By afternoon,
hurricane wings
beat down the door.
A hundred purple eyes danced
in the flaming waves
of a green gold sea.

Now our bird's
in the grip
of a Bengal tiger.
An even match.
Outcome unknown.

Naming the Birds

I dream of burning houses,
mudslides, and rotting flesh.
An old woman stands in the snow
pointing to the branches of a bright green tree.

But my eyes are fixed on the sky,
the T-shaped silhouette of a bald eagle
riding a warm air current,
and what could be a rarer golden
soaring over the garage.

I'm leaning out the window,
showing off how I know these beauties
and recognize them migrating
through my private air space.

The Old One doesn't turn.
She says, "A Wokoki."
So I climb into the cold blue morning
and stand beside her
under drooping leaves dolloped with snow.

I follow her gaze to a feathered gargoyle
camouflaged white on white,
preening itself in the heart of the tree.
The breast is plump like a dove's
and the beak and bedraggled wings
heavy as a stork's.
He scratches his head with a scaly foot,
then dissolves like a cloud.

The Old One's birds reveal themselves
in sifting snow and flashes of dubious taxonomy,
infusing the tree
with shining invisibility.

When I wake in the burned house,
something marvelous and familiar
blooms in the back of my heart.

Passing Through on Your Way

The salty apple smell of your hair
says you are very close this dream night.
When others talk of a new church,
speculate about the bells, their placement,
and the proper way to ring,
I stop listening.
I become a baby
seated on another mother's lap
even as I search for you,
my son come to my old hometown.

I see you standing on the corner,
your hair lit by the street lamp,
the brown suede jacket
we bought at Salvation Army
snug across your back.
You face away,
ready to slip through a gap
in the Nettleton's iron fence.
Why? In all my years,
I never crossed that treeless lawn
or climbed the steps to the shingled house.

I want to call you back
but haven't learned to speak.
I want to run to you
but I am too young to even walk.
I curl my chubby toes
and kick my useless little feet.
I bounce in the arms of the one who holds me.
She thrusts a silver rattle in my fist.
My fingers lock on the cool handle.

My arm swings wildly,
and, like a true bell,
the toy rings
clear high crystal clangs.

Your golden head turns.
Through the singing space of a long time,
your eyes shine into mine.
I laugh and I remember.
Mrs. Nettleton's name is Hope.
Her daughter is Blythe.
It's Easter morning
and you are alive.

Last Night, the Tree of Life

Last night, the Tree of Life
grew beneath my bedroom.
A square black hole
opened like an air shaft in the middle of the floor,
and the room swelled with the scent of cedar and birch,
mushrooms, night rain, and immaculate silence.

I crawled to the edge
and lowered my face into the darkness.
My eyes opened like giant satellite telescopes,
but with no light to receive,
my pupils could only pour their own black ink
into the void.

When I lay my belly on the cool planks
and plunged my arm into the hole,
I could feel the pull of gravity.
The Mother of Matter
was working the muscles of my elbow and wrist.
She massaged my fingers
as if they might sprout roots
and grow to meet the tender crown
of her subterranean living tree.

My dangling arm lost all feeling,
along with my shoulder, cheek, hips and feet.
My whole body turned to stone –
not fossilized like a skeleton
or preserved as footprints in the sand,
but actually dissolved.
In the way a caterpillar disintegrates within the pupa,
I mineralized into rock

without sight, taste, or smell,
language, thought or memory.
Only an elemental stillness,
a communion with the night.

Sophia, Awake in the Middle of the Night

Tonight the world is small.
It fits inside my womb.
I walk through shafts of moonlight
on the painted floor.
Each step rocks my pelvic cradle,
earth bones of oceanic weight.

Once, I was weightless
and rode the blue mare belly down
through bottomless waves of space.
My breastbone fused
to her muscled neck.
My hair tangled in her silver mane.
Galloping was a necessary beauty,
my only task to hold on.

But light became matter.
Mother? Lord?
You delivered me into the earth
and disappeared.

Out of minerals,
I grew monuments to appease you
and invented music to draw you in.
I carried everything
to the top of the mountain,
waiting for the blue mare's return
and calling to you in every language
until my words drifted to dust.

I am pregnant
with accretions of the past.
I need your hurricanes
and lightning fires
to induce this stillbirth.
You need me
to make you holy.

What Is Your Name Before You Are Born?

In a dream, the woman in charge
demanded that I leave the party,
abandon the long-legged daughter
I had been hiding from her,
and enter alone
the white room of her creation.
All night she chased me
through her mansion and formal gardens
crowded with fancy guests.
We were invisible.
I had the girl by the wrist,
the hem of her shirt,
the small of her back.
Under cover of an ancient yew
whose branches, like giant spider legs,
touched down in dry needles,
we crouched skin to skin.
Our electrons exchanged orbits
unseen by the woman in charge,
who kept circling
and calling my name.

Frogs jump onto city streets before an earthquake.
Ants leave their mounds.
I run when the river turns back on itself.

But the painter decides where light must fall.
The tip of her brush separates figure from ground.
My daughter blotted into the shadows.
I felt her hand cool and flatten.
Her fingers slipped from my grip
like a folded paper fan.

I knelt alone on the canvas
where the woman grew wings,
and the primal yew caught fire.

Persephone's Return

1.

She finds me curled, asleep
against the back wall of her shed.
I smell the mud on her boots,
hear the bucket drop,
and her knees creak
as she slips the lavender pillow under my head.
Soon the muslin case is damp
with dribbles of garlic broth, rhubarb honey,
tincture of raspberry root.

My mother is desperate for reunion.
Her medicine spoon opens my lips,
but she cannot make me swallow
or shake off the rude royal armor
of this dreamless sleep.

Half frozen, inert, apart,
I choose to keep my eyes sealed
against her too-bright light
as she tromps the property
with her restless spades and forks,
loppers, plows and pruners.
Her swarms of hungry bees
frantically dancing,
desperate for pollen,
determined to suck the nectar
from every flower,
and feed their honey
to the young.

Even goddesses sometimes wonder
if they got the wrong mother.

2.

As a girl, I snitched an arrow
from Diana's quiver.
I carved a greenwood bow
and stalked a wild boar
into the long shadowed forest.
My mother drew me back from the woods
before the pig caught my scent.

At the abandoned quarry,
I watched a boy jump feet first
into the black pool,
bob to the surface,
his head shining and sleek as a muskrat's,
arms slender, impossibly white,
wavering just under the water
like earthshine cradling a dark moon.

I couldn't wait to plunge through that cold,
but my mother heard the splash,
dove in after,
hauled me up,
laid me out on the slick coal ledge.
She beat the water from my lungs
and filled my body with her breath.

I swam through her eyes
all the way to the place of my beginning.
When her hot tears poured onto my cheeks,
I tasted the salt of an infinite ocean.

3.

Now the quarry's fenced and mostly filled.
The forest clear-cut.

Irrigation ditches dug,
and the bare earth given
to the plant and harvest rhythm
of this world.

Maybe I am home
in these rows of cabbage and strawberry,
sugar beets and flax.
But soon the ground will give way.
Perhaps this summer.
Perhaps the next.
Who can say how many days, weeks,
seasons of everlasting light
must drop like stones in her pockets,
before I save her in my world
like she saved me in hers.

Light Strikes the Bell of the Heart

"You've Reached Peter. Please Leave a Lengthy Message!"

Two weeks of heavy rain.
Ulmer's lower fields
lie plowed and puddled
thick with crows.
Six red calves born this month
are closed in the barn without their mothers.
Back fence rails blew down.
Just beyond Castle Rock,
Durham Creek broke its muddy banks.
Now miniature rivers meander
through the heron rookery
and dissolve in a quiet pool with skunk cabbage islands.
But the creek's main channel is a raceway,
and all the stones are singing
louder than the kestrel's *killy killy*,
the crows, the cows, the gunshot.
I'm telling you, my son,
the lithosphere's alive
in the crash of rock and water,
the noisy harmonics
of clearing and carrying away.

Oriole Nest

A math problem falls out of my bird book.
Faint writing on a square paper
in a hand I don't recognize.
Find the volume of the solid.
Lines that follow are as mysterious to me
as the tablature of bird calls.
But the long *S* hook,
repeating itself down the page,
exactly mimics the broken branch I'm holding.
The smooth cup of parentheses
gathering scratchy little numbers
to be squared, plus and minus,
could be the soft gravid sac,
empty and dangling by its long neck.

Only the oriole knows
how many eggs she laid,
and whether they hatched and flew
before the branch snapped.
But the bird's high clear voice sings
in the warp and weave off milkweed down,
blond hair and indestructible threads
pulled from an old blue tarp.

Here are the sides we can lean against.
Here is the hollow where we will gather.
You and I
far out on the branch of this scarlet oak,
suspended between heaven and earth.

Cerulean Window, Maybe a Door

In the dream,
a small square of blue water quivered
at the end of a black tunnel
in the hold of a ship
overrun by pirates.
I hid among the rough and bloody
carcasses of slaughtered sharks
and mutilated swordfish.

On a walk a few days later,
blue was a sliver of sky,
an opening between two rows of black linden trees,
an early morning invitation
up a steep asphalt road.
I stood at the bottom with my good dog,
each of us breathing and staring up
at the pure color
when light strikes
the bell of the heart.

In Your Shoes

Today I wore your green and brown sneakers
and made tracks in the soft mud of the Birthday Trail,
through Hoffman's Woods and over Wolf Rock.
I kept Ben on the lead across the power cut
and yanked him back from a startled fawn,
all tiny speckled bones and beating heart in the tall grass.

In Ulmer's greening fields, Ben ran free,
sailing over hummocks to the cow pond.
The goslings' mother came on like a jet ski,
but he dodged her and nailed a groundhog
in the ragged rows of corn stubble.

I heard its shrill whistle and click.
Ben's tail flicked up as he pounced.
He shook the creature twice
and flung it high into a wide blue space.
It slowly somersaulted
and arched its back, stroking upward
as if air was water and groundhogs swim.

Maybe they do.
Ben leapt and caught it in his eager jaws.
He bowed and braced his hind legs
and thrashing back and forth,
made his whole body wag
with brute and beautiful delight.
I stood mute as your old shoes,
in miles and miles of missing you.

Coyote's Return

Belled cats lope home
from their hopeless patrols.
Humans pour warm milk,
close curtains,
flood their lawns with artificial light.

Coyote crosses an alley.
She picks her way through the dark,
violent weave of barberry
and climbs the hill of old refrigerators,
smashed up cars, rubber tires and tractor parts.

Wind tastes of lightning.
Smoke-colored clouds
chase the last lavender threads of sunset
over the rooftops and junkyard,
into a stand of sumac trees
whose red velvet seed clumps
flame bright as torches,
then smudge out.

Coyote's eyes hold all the light she needs.
She is the rainmaker.
Sharp-nosed rat catcher.
Star singer.
Tail slinging moonbeam dancer.
Fleet, furred fawn trouncer.

Vultures hunched on the empty silo
spread their wings to welcome her.
Lost dogs yelp and whimper,
begging not to be rescued,
but to breed.

To the Vulture in Search of a Dead Groundhog

Your V-shaped shadow wakes Ben.
He catapults from the porch
and crisscrosses the winter garden,
bursting the seeds of brown-eyed Susan
and barking at the brittle ghosts
of lavender, sage and cosmos.

You circle high above Ben's rising cries.
Do your garnet eyes see
how his whirling body churns the air
that cools your bald head
and lifts your ragged fingered wings?
Is your slow hover
only about a rotting corpse,
or like me, are you caught
in the wide arc of this dog's joy?
The zest of his chase.
The art of his hunt.
The elegance of the kill.

Like a spoon,
Ben stirs everything
in our sky-brimmed earth bowl.

May each one eat
and be full.

Silent Retreat

On the first night,
a junco beat his wings against
our lamp-lit kitchen window.
He wheeled and flashed
a strip of white inside his grey skirts.
The black cowl chest thrust upward,
and his head struck the glass
like a ball peen hammer.
Twice more the window rattled
before we shut the lights
and finished our miso soup in the dark.

Seated in meditation all week,
I felt this warm weightless bird
riding my shoulder.
His delicate clawed feet anchored wide apart.
Wings and tail folded
as he bobbed up and down,
investigating, in rhythm to my breath,
the dry well of my collarbone
and deeper jugular notch.

His beak found the rancid stash of seeds.
With stinging precision,
he cracked the kernels
and filled his crop.

The final night,
I walked with the others,
deliberate, quiet as possible,
circling twice around the backyard.
High above our bowed heads,

I heard the soft whirring chirps
of migrating birds.
The hungry ghost
pushed off my shoulder
and flew to meet his brothers.

Gaia's Prayer

May you discover again the order of things.
After snowdrops, skunk cabbage.
Bloodroot before furry yellow coltsfoot.
Don't even think about morels
until mayapples
open their green umbrellas.

Hard rains fill the lowest places first.
Ditches, gullies and dry runs must flood
before the creek becomes a roiling river,
the hillside a thundering cataract,
the street where you live
a swirling Ahab sea tossed with broken trees.
Next hour, next day when the mailbox is packed with mud,
a brown trout flops on the driveway.
Next week, spinach from your washed-out garden
takes root in your neighbor's lawn.

Take off your boots.
Your gloves.
Your glasses.
Turn out the lights.
Let the animals who taught you
how to feed yourselves
walk through your dreams.

Sleeping All Night on the Dock
for Ben

It was barely autumn in our hemisphere
when winter's Great Dog
dug his last hole
and scrambled onto the horizon.
He snapped up the morsel of moon
and with his bushy tail,
swept the last leaves
from Haystack Mountain.
The moment his paw touched the lake,
the Milky Way slid down his back.
All the stars tumbled in,
but not our bright dog.
His paws never broke the surface.
Not one for swimming,
he walked on the silvery water.
Without a sound
Ben crossed over,
wagging
while I slept.

Windless Night in the Forest

Only trees and me awake.
We strain to listen further out
and hear the stars sing
and the big moon break its suction
when it floats up free.
We want more tonight
than the pumping xylem and the blood.
More than noisy workings
of our different flesh
exchanging breath –
their out, my in,
my out, their in.

Men write books explaining forests
with colored plates of roots and leaves
beneath glassine sheets,
line drawings of cells and stoma,
and cartoon maps of respiration.
Transpiration. Photosynthesis.
As if our sun's the only star we need,
and all the rest are asterisks
at the bottom of the page.

They never ask the trees themselves,
or all of us who breathe
the elemental dust of unnamed stars
and feel night's fathomless fingers
tug our longing limbs,
the generation of our beginning
and our end.

Night Life

For ten years, I slept on the bare ground.
My hips and shoulders saddled
to the swell of the next earthquake.
My face open to the night sky,
waiting for your meteoric return.

Until one morning, a raccoon
crisscrossed the clearing,
skinny as an old grey cat,
tail dragging,
black mask pinched
and torn around the nose.
His vacant eyes met mine.
He slinked away,
but the stare remained,
leaving me small and alone
in a menacing world
where the screech owl's penetrating questions
sounded like accusations,
and the fox's ululating screams
like murderous war cries.

I lost my nerve sleeping out.

Until a forest grew in my dreams,
and you were there.
Not as a falling star,
but yourself,
waking up
in a bright hammock
hung in the highest branch.
You climbed down,

so I returned.

A and B Blown Out to Sea

Arctic Prayer

Let me be
a cobalt blue house
empty as an eggshell
with four windows
undivided and aligned,
two in front
and two in back,
so a child
trudging to school
on a snowbound morning
can stare through me
twice
at the roiling sea.

After a Great Storm

The wild horsewoman turns,
her flaming hooves in smoky retreat,
barely a gallop
across the soot-smeared skin
of her animal drum.
She slows to a four-beat amble
and melts into the unfurling light.

The raven freezes midflight
against a bank of clouds.
His wings collapse
like a broken umbrella
and he drops,
an inkblot tumbling
off a fresh page,
a pinging submarine scream
peeling the ocean
off the jagged lava rocks.

Remember when air was water?
Our hollow gourd earth
bobs in the frigid surf,
and the raven
is still on the wing.

Endless as an Arctic Winter Night

Tell us a story
that will put us to sleep.
Let your words fall
like our grandmother's thick shank of hair
when she opens the ivory clasp
and her rough fingers start unbraiding,
and her soft brush
smooths the black cascade
over the mountain of her shoulders,
releasing every speck
of dry grass, flecks of birch bark,
tobacco snuff, fish scales and cattail fluff
in tiny puffs
that catch the yellow lantern light,
and floating,
spin more stories
no one ever hears
to the end.

Winter's Wise Counsel

When the blue night rushes in,
you find yourself
blind and deaf
as a newborn pup.
Snow sprays buckshot
on your face and shoulders,
heaps dunes on your boots,
and freezes the oxygen out of the air.
Wind hammers ice nails into your teeth,
and scores a message
on your corneas –
Forget about straight-line walking.
A and B
have blown out to sea.
Bow your head.
Stumble home.
Some oil remains
in the lamp
on the sideboard.
Yesterday
you boiled an egg,
still unbroken
in its shell.

Night Before the Last Ship Sailed

Some mighty god forged this blue steel helmet,
smelting earth iron in dragon fire,
and studding the breast plate
with sapphire stars
that flash winter light.

The guard who wears this armor
stands erect, high above the harbor
on a jagged, black columned cliff.
His back to the village,
he keeps watch on the vanishing horizon.

No one told his mute daughter.
She crawls through the dry grass
and onto the toes of her father's heavy boots.
She plays in the folds of his deerskin cloak.
He is not easily distracted.
She does not easily give up,
tugging and twisting the hem
until he finally feels,
yields, stoops
and lifts the blue-eyed girl
off the earth.

Maybe you've watched
her fingers tangle his icy beard
and kiss his midnight cheek.
Maybe you've felt
the sweeping tenderness when he bends again.
Reluctance
when he lays her down to sleep.
All without leaving his post,
the moon and the night command.

We Are More and Less Than We Know, and Braver Too

Tonight the tide is out, Isabella.
The black sand beach belongs to your red galoshes,
your legs running, your mother's voice
small and smaller beyond the tangled nets,
kelp and broken floats,
over the dunes
to the wide frosted sea wash,
clean as a Sunday morning street,
empty save the sleek silver spotted body
of a harbor seal
swept in by the moon.

Your palm strokes the cold fur-bolstered torpedo.
Your fingers trace the ridges in her flipper tail,
and fused leather hands.
Ear vents feel like holes in a whistle.
Pincushion cheeks sprout wire whiskers
and a nose like your brother's in a broad flat face.
The grey blue eyes un-alive,
hold almond pieces of the winter sky
with specks of you
in your yellow pompom hat.

Not so long ago, the edge of your perception
was the kitchen doorway.
You knelt on all fours
to cross the transom like a pup,
then rose and toddled
toward the sea.

Early Morning in the Studio

Stillness on the snow-banked land.
Houses and the school
heaped together like sleeping polar bears,
while out beyond the charcoal line of sea,
clouds and mountains spar
in jealous competition for the light.
Retreat. Advance. Reconfigure.
These rivals can't keep themselves intact.
Ice and rock may as well
be mist and air.
Old as the mountains are,
named and marked with trails,
their shapes cannot hold.
Don't they know?
Light decides who stays and goes.
Like a beggar with an empty bowl,
the wise eye waits and knows.

Song of the Hag

Don't mistake ice for death.
Inertia for sterility.
Your meager senses cannot fathom
the primeval forest impounded in this heart
and fed these thousand years on desire,
without water, light, or air.

You have dug me up,
plucked me from my frozen rocky home.
I am discovered –
What will you do?

Fling me out to the distant ocean?
I swear I will barnacle myself
to the bottom of any boat you try to sail.
I will cling to the rudder
and turn your skiff forever in my direction.

Will you crush, burn, or cut me?
Try, if you must. I will not die.
Go ahead. Dissect and study.
Fix the thinnest slice to a slide.
You'll detect no parts.
Only a solid mystery
the lamps of your microscope
can never penetrate.

Or will you carry me home,
plant me in your own moist soil,
let my roots grow into your flesh,
and my stem climb through your throat?

Will you let the long journey
out from yourself
finally bloom?

Last Day on Hrísey

Sometimes the cold sky gets trapped in its own glare.
The bay turns white
as the old snow mountains,
and the island loses all its edges.
Even the clock on the wall
can't keep time to itself.
So I grab my boots
and tramp down to the village pool
to lounge in the steam
and half float like a seal
among pink-fleshed men and women.

Friends speak softly to one another,
with lilting r's and o's and s's
in syllables I hear as music.
When the young fish factory girl
spots a flock of snow buntings
flying over our icy heads,
everyone hushes,
and we lift our faces
toward a sound like rain.
The tiny striped wings pump the air.
They move as one flashing body,
a wave that twists and curls in on itself,
sifts onto a nearby rooftop,
rises, and disintegrates like smoke
to reconfigure in some unpredictable place.

I don't know the Icelandic words
for the grey wake
that stretches out and vanishes
behind the ferry I ride out of here.
Bless Bless means goodbye
to the birds
and whispering sky.

From Earth to the Separating Stars

To the Grandchildren

Clocks will try to convince you
every moment is divisible
by every other moment.
And scales say a pound of flesh
is just as heavy as a pound of feathers.
But the distance between two people
is not a straight line,
any more than the moon
is a landing pad for Mars.

One day you may see the film by Eames –
a couple unwrapping sandwiches
on the grassy shore of Lake Michigan.
A checkered cloth, a wine bottle,
his hand, hers.
The camera pulls back ten meters.
The couple shrinks.
Ten times ten times ten,
the lens ever widening,
and the skyscrapers flattening,
as the big city
becomes a motherboard
on the cuff of a grey mitten.
The planet a blue marble.
Then a speck of dust.
Gone.

Don't be fooled by the long darkness
or blinded by the speed of light.
No one can be lost in a universe
invented by love
and played in pat-a-cake
on a blue and purple quilt.

Here, Now

Your body lay in a long, plain pale box.
We read a Wendell Berry poem.
Mr. Wally Long lowered the lid gently.

Yet, days later you walked behind me
on the frozen path to Cory's
and spoke in your clear full voice,
"Mom! I have your back!"

Who but the bearer speaks to the truth inside feeling?

Each year on newly risen scapes, the snowdrops do.
Their pearl heads lie down
in the place you must have stood.
I pick them and remember
your hand on my right shoulder,
your strong, flat-tipped fiddler fingers
and the thumb you sucked when you were small.
Your cheek and breath against my cold ear.
All of you, every impossible cell,
actual living flesh,
past, present – yes, some future –
pressed upon me then and there.

I dreamt of you before your birth.
I never dream you died,
only that you're sometimes traveling,
or disguised as a child
or turning into an eagle.

I thought there were so many snowdrops
here that spring.
Far more have gone and come up since.
As if I need to be convinced.

Evidence

The child may go away to school
or move to another country,
even be sent to the penitentiary,
but he sleeps in his parents' house,
his heartbeat set to the ticking furnace.

Death says, *Ah, but this is different.*
Knowing the body well,
with maps and medical reports,
Death files an affidavit on the boy
and tries to send him off
to the real estate of heaven.

It's not mother love or wishful thinking
that rejects Death's claim.
It's the testimony of a spider
in the empty bedroom corner,
who saw the light flash on then off,
and a little grey moth
who rode the son's shoulder
as he tiptoed past his sleeping parents,
down the stairs, out the latched door.

He crossed the moonlit yard
just as the barn owl, in her silent hunt,
pumped upward from the shadows.
He made his way to the highway
and paused to light a cigarette
by the entrance ramp,
in streaming headlights
of long distance trucks.

Death says, *That boy never smoked.*

Yes, but the blind possum saw,
and the mockingbirds are witness.
Even now, many times in many places,
they know the truth
and sing it all night long.

Prayer of the People

*"When the thing is born,
born of yourself, born."*
— Charles Olson

Where do we begin?
When the soul is forged in the expanding universe?
When our mother dreams us into the ocean of her body?
Or that quickening leap, zing, and tumble
against the chambers of her heart?

Storm surge. Flood tide.
We fall into our father's arms
and take our place
in the ancestral line
of ordinary time.
First words. First steps.
We answer to our given name
and learn how to belong.

We are like trees rooting to the shore,
like shushing grasses lulled by wind,
unaware of the mute grey spider
who moves among us
casting her luminous thread.

That each might bear
the weight of her filament
and be bound by its resonance.
One to another,
through endless blind beginnings
and broken cords,
our lives become a hymn
from earth
to the separating stars.

Ocarina

Love, I recognize the gag.
That routine perfected
the summer you were four –
box in a box in a box,
each one wrapped and ribboned
tighter than the last.
I could never open fast enough.
You could never keep the secret till the end,
blurting out when you saw my interest fade
in the face of all that duct tape,
"It's a feather!" or
"I made it out of Alice's tooth!"

No tape now. No paper.
I opened the door.
Two troopers held their hats
and a little card penciled
with the misspelled name of a mountain
that swallowed you.

The television was on.
Some hearty Italian lady poured wine
into a marinara anyone could make.

Across the ocean,
you were separating from your body,
lifting out of time.
pouring or floating
– even rocketing –
into space.

I found your paper-mâché mask
with the bone nose,
the chair built of deer scapula, grapevine and antler,
the topo map of coyote sightings.
I made the troopers touch these things
and stand in the living room
while I blew into the owl-shaped ocarina
that takes two hands to hold.
Each time, I said, "Here is Peter!"
"Here is Peter!"
"Here is Peter!"

And after the troopers
and your father and your sisters,
I told the dog, the snowdrops,
red-winged blackbirds,
certain clouds, rocks, wind, mountains
and Brahms,
played over and over
till I can sing the requiem
by heart
and open more.

About That Thought Experiment by Schrödinger

*"If all the little particles follow quantum mechanics,
and everything is made of little particles, then shouldn't
all the big things follow quantum mechanics?"*
  – *Physicist Aaron O'Connell*

Let's say, no one's home
when the two policemen knock.
Cat out. Lights out.
I have chosen to join my husband
at the evening service,
grab a pizza on the Southside,
and after all these years,
spring for the late late Rocky Horror.

Once you start looking for particles,
time and space collapse.
Think about waves,
and everyone keeps dancing.

But as I understand this,
nobody has to dance.
Just stay away.
Let the policemen
go back where they came from.

Easy as breathing,
Saturday dissolves into Sunday.
6:40 AM in Zurich, Switzerland,
a train departs for Paris.
A bowlegged conductor
dressed almost like a policeman
lopes down the aisle.
Swaying in place, he clicks the ticket
of an American teenager.
A diamond-shaped particle falls away.

That's it.
No mountain. No snow.
No upside down green snowboard.
Just that tiny hole
snipped through the paper ticket
registered in his name,
and the drowsy boy,
cradling a fiddle on his lap,
rides the high-speed train
all the way to the end.

Mudstone Speaks to the Mother of Matter

You say, Tell me the Truth.
Yet in the next breath, you insist
we begin at the Beginning.
This can only send us straight
to the biggest lie of all –
The End.

Don't you know?
Animal, vegetable, mineral
cannot escape the infinite Middle
of the never-ending, ever-forming
All.

You say, Once upon a time, a boy.
Why not twice?
Why not always or never?

Only a fool would try to distinguish a boy
from a mountain.
A snowflake from a star.
An avalanche. A constellation.

Love named the boy.
Conceived the Big Bang,
and started the clock
inside your body.

As if there were no mountain.
No limestone, feldspar,
and mighty crystals of calcite and amethyst
uplifting Mägis Alp,
while many miles deep within,
the mudstone quietly dissolves.

Mudstone doesn't battle gravity.
Even as a chunk is torn from the rest,
river-carved, collapsed
and dragged through crooked passageways,
to land at the feet of some old hag
who dares to call herself a maker,
we abide.

She climbs on top of us,
and we smell her animal skins
and hear the blood rush
through her mighty legs.

She wields the wind in her diamond blade.
Magnetism in the full weight of her dream.

Particles hang in the air,
settle into the cracks of floor and walls.
Our dust fills her throat
and coats her hair and skin,
but her eyes are clear.

Every mud-made muscle is her creation.
Every numbered hair and freckle
her design, her conviction
as she wrestles with the heavy pants,
zippered jacket, woolen hat
and stiff black boots.

We are the body she dresses
and buries head down
in three meters of fresh snowfall
on the side of the mountain.
The body dragged and lifted
into a spruce box,

carried through the sky,
across the ocean to America.

The one you weep over,
pray over, mourn,
burn, and bury
twenty-eight inches deep
in Nisky Hill Cemetery.

We hear your footsteps
and the click of pebbles and sticks
in the little basket you carry.
When you kneel by the granite marker
and start to build a fairy house,
we feel the full weight of Mägis Alp
bearing down on the impossible physics
of any beginning
that could ever bring us
to the end.

The Message

Make me your livery boy.
I will lead your steed
down from the far forgotten pasture,
and guide her by halter
across the gravel paddock
to the stable's shafted light.

Wait there.
I'll prepare her for your journey –
trim the cracked hooves with my farrier knife,
curry the matted coat and braid ribbons
in her long silver mane.
I'll slide the bit in her mouth and anoint.

I have found the secret hoard
of summer's golden yield
and lashed seven ladders
to stash it in the topmost loft.
She will eat this grain.

I have hiked seven mountains
to reach the sweetest glacial spring.
She will drink this water.

The crimson robe falls across her back.
You ride with no saddle.
Seize the reins firmly.
Let your body be still.
Lean into her with all your being.

She is not the sweetest,
but, Mom, she is the best.
She can take you to the stars.

Guaranteed.

Not Yet

I watch for the wild blue mare
haltered on Mägis Alp,
watered at the Reutibach,
curried, brushed and fed
a thousand days.

You tell me she is mine to ride,
trained in bareback just for me,
but oh, my darling,
do not say free,
and not alone. Not yet.

Please stay a little while.

Walk her round the lighted stable once
so I can hear the rhythm of her natural gait.
Draw her near. Dispel my terror
of muscled winged desire
and clattering hooves that paw the air.

Make your hands a stirrup for my foot.
Hoist me up and climb on too.
With arms around this graceless rider's waist,
guide our midnight horse.

As I did, many years ago,
seated on a sled
with you tucked in ahead,
my chin on your crown,
my mother-hands the reins.
So fast we flew
and down.

Old Love Knits a Sweater

Here in the City

The radiator makes the sound of wild geese.
I am awake,
watching flakes of snow or tiny stars
drift down from the cracked ceiling
and melt into my dark quilt.
This flock of birds comes from some other dark.
Their honks and barks and hollow jangles
are faint and far away,
but a last, long reed cry
slips through the window.
The room fills with creamy white silence.
Feather shadows float across the walls.
Liquid wings with fingers
open, fold and open.
These are faint impressions,
sepia ink images that barely hold together
until I hear them breathing.
There must be hundreds of them.
Like a giant loom working warp and weave
in an old dusty factory,
this breath works the wings of my heart.

I think of you all the time.
Not the nineteen-year-old.
As you said in one of our dreams,
"Mom. I'm not just one thing."

Old Love Knits a Sweater

The moon drops.
It lands with a soft plunk.
and breath unravels
its royal blue line.

I knit and pearl
downhill,
according to the pattern
scrimshawed on my bones.

The sweater hangs
too long at the wrists
too wide at the waist.
Still I feel your elbows
poking through
whenever I drop a stitch
and your broad back
splitting the seams.

Soft wool
can never hold you.
But neither will I stop
my craft
to ever let you go.

Time Travel

All night I rode in a cream-colored Buick
with chrome circled gauges on a glossy wooden dash.
I sat alone in the back seat
as the dream maker drove us into the sea.

Now I meet you at the breakfast table
of daytime abstractions.
Words and money. Husband and wife.
Coffee and steel-cut oats.
Raisins taste like nails that rust my teeth.
Maybe yours, too.
I don't ask about your body.
You don't look at mine.

In the newspaper, the world comes apart
in neat sections.
Yours and mine. Us and them.
You notice road repairs on Route 412
and plan another way to keep from losing time.

I want to ask, why save Time?
Isn't Time the one who stole our boy?
We keep blaming the mountain,
the quality of the snow,
the slope, gravity, velocity –
But really, if not for Time,
he could be sitting between us,
pouring milk into the yellow bowl.

If I look up from the front-page story
of refugees tossed in a leaden sea,
I see only you, through micro molecules

of salt water flooding my eyes.
You, drowning in your own Aegean Ocean,
your private boat as broken as mine by the gale.
And then what?

You leave for work and I come to the part
about twenty-nine bodies washed up on a beach.
The Red Crescent rushes to retrieve the dead
while they still have faces.

I remember my dream ride in the Buick,
the creaking springs coiled under cool worn leather,
the dashboard with its spinning needles.
Every meter, compass and clock
searches wildly for home.

I want to tell you of the moment
my bare foot kicked back the duvet.
I want to ask what you dream
when the spiral eye gathers you in.

Animal Soul Longing

I wish you could see the spider
I feel jazz dancing in my ear,
her long jointed legs
lifting and dipping her two-part body
like a Javanese shadow puppet.

I wish you would come close enough
to reach the weir of my rib cage
and touch the flailing tail of the golden salmon
caught and raised so far from the river,
she's forgotten how to swim.
Leap! She tells me. *Now!*
It kills her that I don't.

Sometimes I feel fur
between you and me.
Thick velvet pelts flash orange
when we meet nose to nose,
tracking the same faint ley line
in opposite directions.

Other times I see crows
gather in your eyes,
beating their wings,
tormenting the kestrel circling in mine.

Or is it the other way around?
I wish you would tell me
who jumps over your brain
and dozes in your belly.
Is there a pool where a dragonfly drinks?

The Union of Two Rays at a Vertex

38 years to write a love poem,
and still no words.
Page after page of numbers
describe the obtuse,
side angle side geometries
we try to approximate.
But the figure cannot close
as long as one plus one
keeps making five.

I am an expert in addition,
slow to subtract,
and division is a long labor
of trial and error
before you can bring down.
Our toes and fingertips
stretch in opposite directions.
We strive for infinite distances,
while the same variable
on both sides
divides by itself
and cancels out.

Left at the Altar of Undigested Light

To the fox who saw me first
and froze the moment
with his cryogenic gaze,
I was a woman in flannel pajamas
swinging her bucket of scraps
as she hurried to the compost heap.

I was writing a letter
when the smudged point of his tail
split the morning in two parts.

The larger piece,
a whirling circus trick on black-stocking stilts.
A ruddy fur flame
that rippled over the snow swept field
and vanished in a miracle of light between the trees.

He left me there to breathe
the air he breathed
and play the smaller part,
pouring out my meager offering
of vegetable peelings, lettuce ribs
leek leaves and walnut shells.

All the roots and stems too tough
for human mouths to chew and swallow
scattered on the frozen earth,
along with the apples we'd let rot in the bowl.
Deep gold and luminous.
Their soft bruised flesh
so fragrant.

Returning to the Labyrinth After Weeks in the City

Ignore the twigs and leaf litter,
sprouts of clover and stilt grass,
toppled rocks and chipmunk holes.
Leave the scat a fox or raccoon
deposited on the slab of Indiana greenstone.

The labyrinth's not a house you're cleaning
or a problem you are solving.
It's not your private project,
your journey, or your silent prayer.

You walk this stage
for the pleasure of the red-bellied woodpeckers
who police this corner of the forest
and jackhammer dead trees.
Now, with their nest empty
and stomachs full of emerald ash borers,
the bright capped couple
perches in the green branches.
He, in the little tulip poplar to the east,
and she, in the sassafras to the west.
They are studying the creases in your straw hat
and waiting for the show to start –
that slow dance you do
toe to toe, with your long shadow
leading or following,
going nowhere slowly.

Where the Old Dog Dozed

You keep asking,
"She opens the gate?"
"She closes the gate?"
as if this galaxy we inhabit
were a walled city
built by the telescope
and the clock. Tick tock
in a universe unbecoming.

Listen. There is no gate!
Each of us hurries to the wedding
through a labyrinth built from stones
the Lover dug and discarded.
Our footsteps are flowers
trailing fireweed.
Blue smoke from the burning veil
coats the mirror.

Once the old dog dozed
in the space between us.
Now a pool of light
no stitch in time can save.
Gravity holds us in this moment.
She has threaded our needles
and bowed our heads.
What can we do
but sit and mend
our little lives?

Maybe This Is Why I Married You

The notion that we might be born again
comforts. Then terrifies. Then thrills
like a landlocked lake back in Ohio.
Conceived by an engineer,
born from a dammed creek
and 650 acres of pasture and Adena Indian graves,
Cowan Lake was just a couple years older than me,
and already famous
for lightning strikes with no thunder
and crazy gusts of strong wind
that dropped down from the limestone cliffs
and bounced around like pinballs.
Champion sailors loved to race
with spinnakers puffed,
skippers and mates hiking out
to keep their sleek boats stable,
ready to come about the course
set by the Race Committee that very morning.

I was eleven years old,
suspicious of speed,
clueless about tell-tails,
and bored with the strategies of winning anything.
The open water unnerved me,
but I had the good fortune
of a tiny flat-bottomed wooden dinghy
impossible to capsize,
and I chose to love the lake
not for her shiny shifting surface,
but for everything she hid.

All that summer, I sailed in and out a quiet cove
where tree trunks stood like stranded swimmers
and me, bobbing over the rippling surface,
poking the lake bottom with a long stick,
hoping for clay pipes and carved birds
wampum beads, or – Imagine! –
a skull.

I try to place you there,
growing up in small-town Ohio
instead of New Jersey.
Probably seated at a picnic table
high above the lake,
somewhere between the parking lot and pavilion.
You, hunkered down behind a stack of encyclopedias,
would never see the girl
marching past in wet sneakers,
her jean shorts bulging
with stones and rusty fishing lures,
a black snake comfortably slung about her neck.
And I, in that life,
never glance back over my shoulder
to see the *Tom Swift* book that boy is actually reading,
or the calculations he's frantically scribbling
to reconcile gravity
with the speed of light,
for a possible rocket ship journey
to Andromeda.

It couldn't happen in that life.
But somehow it still could
in this one.

Field Assistant

Those weeks in southern Greenland,
we walked on top of trees.
Sank knee-deep in forests of creeping juniper
that stained our pants with fragrant oil.
We twisted our ankles
on lichen-crusted crowns of miniature birch
whose brittle underbranches
snapped beneath our galumphing boots.

The scientists were sampling
the oldest bedrock on the planet.
I was drawing pictures
of icebergs floating in the fjord,
and gathering firewood for still nights
when the stars don't show
and fog swallows the aurora.

An armload of broken birch chunks
burns for nearly an hour.
The vertical river of red and orange
sparks, whistles and crackles
as it shoots up to heaven and snuffs out.

Then the darkness
that has been floating over our heads
descends and waits,
like a stranger standing
just outside our little circle.

I wish we knew an ancient ceremony
to honor her.
A holy story to draw her close.

A chant to fill her begging bowl.
But our quick bright fire's gone out,
leaving us shy and ashamed
of all we feel and cannot know.

So we listen for the scrape of an iceberg
nudging the shore.

Ipiutaq, Greenland

All the psalms learned by heart
sound like knock-offs,
and the words of my own invention
are dollar-store wine glasses
teetering on pretentious stems.
I keep drinking new information,
pouring out a thousand convincing story lines,
arranging causes for every effect.
Still, I haven't built a scaffold
high enough to hang You.

I never asked for a lover.
Only an iron mother
to smack that face on the kitchen wall
and keep the long and short
hands ticking.

But You keep playing
the timeless roar of a high waterfall
in the channels of my ear.
A spit of land above a fjord.
The fire doused.
All the geologists asleep in their tents
while the black torrent
washes away their snores.

I stood alone on the permafrost
when the strings of Your robe untied at my throat.
The night sky tore open.
Fields of stars vanished
behind rippling curtains of pale light.
Green and purple flares

fluoresced in swirls of other colors
too fleeting to separate.
Ropes of ether arose in one nowhere,
and unraveled to skeins of nothing in another.

I couldn't hear my heart beat.
Couldn't feel my feet.
Who can say
if my mouth opened,
when the wine of the universe
poured down?

Acknowledgments

I want to thank Diane Frank for teaching me and Blue Light Press – the Editorial Board, book angels, and artistic designer, Melanie Gendron – for publishing this book. I am also grateful to Diane for first publishing some of these poems in *Dreams and Blessings*, and *Pandemic Puzzle Poems*.

The women in my Blue Light Press Poetry Workshop: Suzanne Dudley, Lisha Garcia, Jennifer Read Hawthorn, Nancy Lee Melmon, and Angie Minkin were the first readers of most of these poems. I am grateful for the inspiration and learning that happen when we meet each other on the page.

For the most part, I paint, draw and doodle my way into poems. Residencies at NES and Old School in Iceland, Wellspring House in Massachusetts, and Lacawac in Pennsylvania, refreshed my spirit in the company of so many adventurous artists.

Poems can grow from dark places. Linda Dench helps me discover the vitality and healing energy of the psyche. I am indebted to her for insisting that the path laid down by the dream maker in the night is the only one worth taking through the day.

Finally, I am indebted to Ken Kodama and the close friends and family members around whom I orbit. For all the times you've watched me slip away and all the ways you welcome me when I come circling back: thank you.

About the Author

Anna Kodama writes and paints in eastern Pennsylvania, a few miles from the Delaware River. She has raised children, chickens, and vegetables, and taught adult and family literacy. As "Anna Carr," she authored several books about organic gardening. She is a coauthor of *Dreams and Blessings: Six Visionary Poets*, also published by Blue Light Press.

www.ingramcontent.com/pod-product-compliance
Lightning Source LLC
Chambersburg PA
CBHW031157160426
43193CB00008B/402